DATE DUE

DEMCO 38-296

Into the Volcano

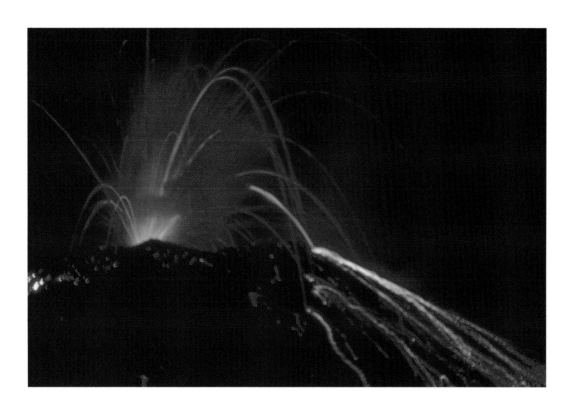

Donna O'Meara
Photographs by Stephen and Donna O'Meara

Kids Can Press

This book is dedicated to my husband, Steve, who is my eternal flame. And to Pele, Mandy and Milky Way, whose everlasting love inspires and guides me. And to my Mom, the truly brave one.

AUTHOR'S NOTE

I have made every effort to present the science of volcanoes accurately, while generalizing some complex geological processes for the benefit of young readers. Different individuals, volcanologists and geologists may use different terms for the same features and processes.

I do not encourage anyone to take risks at volcanoes. All volcanoes are dangerous and unpredictable. There is no sure way to know when or how or where a volcano will erupt catastrophically.

Kids Can Press acknowledges the financial support of the Government of Ontario, through the Ontario Media Development Corporation's Ontario Book Initiative; the Ontario Arts Council; the Canada Council for the Arts; and the Government of Canada, through the BPIDP, for our publishing activity.

Published in Canada by
Kids Can Press Ltd.
29 Birch Avenue
Toronto, ON M4V 1E2

Published in the U.S. by
Kids Can Press Ltd.
2250 Military Road
Tonawanda, NY 14150

www.kidscanpress.com

Technical editor: Stephen James O'Meara
Edited by Valerie Wyatt
Designed by Julia Naimska
Interior illustrations by Céleste Gagnon
Printed and bound in Singapore

This book is smyth sewn casebound.

CM 05 0 9 8 7 6 5 4 3 2 1

National Library of Canada Cataloguing in Publication Data

O'Meara, Donna, 1954–
    Into the volcano : a volcano researcher at work / Donna O'Meara.

Includes index.
For children aged 8–12.
ISBN 1-55337-692-7

1. Volcanoes — Juvenile literature. 2. O'Meara, Donna, 1954– Juvenile literature. I. Title.

QE521.3.D65 2005   j551.21   C2004-902242-3

Kids Can Press is a /©rus™ Entertainment company

ACKNOWLEDGMENTS
This book couldn't have happened without the help of many others. Thanks to:

My husband Steve for his gorgeous photographs and editing; David Bieber for true friendship; Pele, Mandy, Milky Way and Daisy for their magic.

Our dedicated field assistants Tippy D'Auria, Bob Benward, Larry Mitchell, Scott Ireland and Chris Cobb-Smith. Katia Krafft for inspiration. Editor Val Wyatt. Geologist Steve Mattox for reviewing the science.

Sam Pinkus, my agent, for his belief in this project. His sons, Eli and Gabriel, for their volcano enthusiasm.

My sister, Lori Walrath; Mike; Kristin; Vin; Sheila; John; Annette; Gary; France; Mom and Dad.

Eternally to friends at The National Geographic Society for their lasting support: Leslie Schwerin, Nancy Donnelly, Howard Shack, Federico Pucci, Paul Spillanger, Margaret Burnette, MaryAnne Culpepper, Rebecca Martin, Carsten Peter, Jonathan Blair, Jennifer Vernon, Brian Handwerk, Gil Pimental, Tom Foreman, Peter Miller, Lisa Thomas, Anne Williams, Don and Annie Griffith Belt, Mark Christmas, Chris Scaptura and Diana Sperrazza.

Hugs to volcano friends Christina Lieberman, David Okita, Andrea, Edgar Castro, Rolando Benitez, Adrianna Sherman, Dr. Eddie Sanchez, Alfredo McKenny, Otoniel Matias, Sonia Calvari, Rosanna Verladita, Danielle, Lorenzo, Mario, Luka, Elicier Duarte, Little Brother and Sister Edwin, Imelda and Mommy, the Smithsonian Global Volcanism Network staff, Christina Heliker, David, Wendee and Beagle Levy, Rick Fienberg, Kelly Beatty, Dan Greene, Steve Gerrard, Stacey Goldman, John Baptiste, Jeannette and Luc Morel, Alain and Marie Gerente, Jim Quiring, Tim Ferris, Len Bloch, Faelyn Jardine, Tui De Roy, Wolfgang Mueller, Amos and Charlene Meyers, Craig and Arlene Maxey, Andy and Vickie Chaikin, Maxine Kaluna Ohana, Nona and Kaliko Beamer, Susan Stubbs, Amy Evans, Bronwyn and Rikki Cooke, Bill and Pat Ritter, the critters, Myra McClarey, Brad Pitt and Jim Martin. All the world's volcanoes for being being so merciful. Especially Pele.

If I have forgotten to thank anyone please forgive me. I believe my memory may have become addled from inhaling volcanic fumes for so many years, and I do apologize.

Contents

Some Like It Hot

Hawaii's Kilauea
volcano rumbles
under my feet with
thunder I feel in my
stomach. The air reeks of
burning metal. A towering
dark steam cloud looms
over me. Without warning,
a football-sized chunk of
gooey lava drops out of the
cloud and plops onto the
ground near me. I duck and
run as more hissing red
chunks splatter everywhere.
These "lava bombs" could
crush a skull as if it were an
eggshell. What on Earth am
I doing here, on the world's
most active volcano?

When molten hot lava
meets cold ocean water,
explosions blast chunks
of lava up into the air.
Heads up when the chunks
start coming back down!

5

There were no volcanoes where I grew up. Our family lived in a quiet, little town in rural New England where the cows outnumbered the people. I was the eldest of three children and spent my childhood exploring the forests and fields.

My favorite pastime was sitting safe and dry on our porch watching violent summer thunderstorms rage through the Connecticut River Valley. Our springer spaniel, Dinney, would cower under my chair in fright, but the louder the thunder and brighter the lightning, the more thrilled I was.

In school I loved earth science and biology, but my guidance counselor suggested I take typing classes and become a secretary. That didn't interest me. Fortunately, I was artistic, so instead I majored in creative arts — painting, photography and writing. To this day I still can't type.

Does this look like a future volcano researcher?

This photo was taken in the cow pasture behind my parents' house. No volcanoes there!

I've always been artistic. Now I use my camera instead of a paintbrush.

In the 1970s I moved to Boston and worked for magazine and book publishers. But something was missing in my life. Although getting out into the countryside helped, I finally decided I had to make some changes. I wanted to learn about the earth and the sky and the stars, where they all came from and where they were going.

At age 32, I went back to college. My teacher, Stephen James O'Meara, opened my eyes to science when he described how our solar

What can I say? I like silly things.

system was shaped by geological forces. One of the most dynamic forces, Steve said, was volcanism. I pictured Earth, with its 1500 or more volcanoes spewing lava, as it spun dizzily around our sun.

Steve studied volcanoes to learn how planets formed and to search for clues that might help predict when a volcano will erupt here on Earth. So far, no single scientific method can accurately predict deadly eruptions. Any new discoveries would be important scientifically and could save lives.

Steve's daring tales of exploring erupting volcanoes held me spellbound. When he passed around a piece of rough, hardened lava, I held it tight, closed my eyes and imagined myself climbing an erupting volcano in an exotic foreign country. Now that sounded like a good job for me!

Weeks after class ended, Steve and I had dinner. He described how he'd once jumped over a moving lava flow to save his life. I could barely believe what I was hearing. Asleep that night I dreamed of volcanoes.

On December 23, 1986, around noon, my office phone rang. It was Steve.

"Donna, have you ever seen an erupting volcano?"

No, of course I hadn't.

"I'm on my way to Kilauea and need a field assistant."

"Kilauea, Hawaii? When do we leave?"

I said "aloha" to my magazine boss and was on a plane to Hawaii before sunset that same night.

Katia Krafft

The two most important influences on my work have been my husband and research partner, Steve O'Meara, and a volcanologist named Katia Krafft.

Katia got her first taste of volcanoes as a teenager, when her family visited Italy's Stromboli volcano. She was determined to become a volcanologist (a scientist who studies Earth's volcanoes) and did. Along the way she met and married another volcanologist, Maurice Krafft.

Katia's delicate appearance belied her physical strength and courage. Between 1971 and 1991, she dodged lava bombs at Iceland's Eldfell volcano, walked giant earth cracks at Hawaii's Mauna Loa volcano, climbed into erupting Piton de la Fournaise volcano on Reunion Island and inhaled lung-searing gases at countless volcanoes. She even rowed a raft across an acid lake at Indonesia's Kawah Idjen volcano, taking samples until the acid ate away the skin on her hands.

After twenty years at nearly 200 erupting volcanoes, Katia seemed invincible. But on June 3, 1991, while photographing eruptions at Japan's Mount Unzen volcano, Katia and Maurice were engulfed and killed in a pyroclastic flow (see page 29).

I was shocked by the news. In some small way I hope that Steve and I are able to carry on and contribute to the kind of work that was important to the Kraffts.

My First Volcano

At noon on December 24, 1986, Steve and I strapped ourselves into a helicopter without doors and bounced on air drafts over a sizzling Hawaiian lava lake.

The lake had formed when a new vent, called Kupaianaha, had burst open on the east side of Kilauea volcano. A vent is an opening through which a volcano erupts lava and ash from inside the Earth.

Lava oozed out of the vent, filling a huge depression to overflowing and creating a lava lake. The lava gushing into the lake from the vent caused sloshing waves.

As our pilot tilted the chopper to give us a better view, I clutched at the seat cushion for fear I would slide across the smooth leather and right out the open door. Below us a red lake the size of two football fields bubbled like a pot of oatmeal. Only this wasn't oatmeal. It was burning hot molten lava.

Hovering over Kupaianaha lava lake was the scariest thing I'd ever done — until we landed near it.

Explosive Facts

Name of volcano: Kilauea

Location: Hawaii, U.S.A.

Status: active

Type: shield volcano

Height: 1222 m (4009 ft.)

Known people killed: about 120

Closer to the lava lake
things got even scarier. The
lava bubbled up, cooling
into flying spatter
and cinders.

At one end of Kupaianaha lava lake we could see the tube into which lava gushed as it drained from the lake.

Helicopters take volcano hunters where the action is. This one approaches a smoking crater. It's similar to the one we took to see the lava lake — only our chopper didn't have doors!

The chopper whirled down to the edge of the sizzling lake. Hot, glowing rock oozed from the earth like toothpaste out of a cracked tube. The helicopter cabin got hotter, and a burnt metal smell filled the air. Our pilot expertly dodged chunks of spatter the volcano flung at us. We landed on the ground with a soft thump.

Steve and the pilot jumped out and ducked the rotors, leaving the engine running for a fast getaway. I thought about the gasoline in the engine near this heat.

I watched as Steve walked right up to the creeping lava flow — and survived. The scientist in me said "Hey, isn't this what you went back to school for?" The artist in me had to admit the lake was strangely beautiful. Glowing pinkish-orange lava was creeping along, hissing and popping as if it were alive. This was the opportunity I had been waiting for my whole life. I grabbed my camera and jumped out of the chopper. I felt heat through the soles of my sneakers. I changed lenses and started shooting.

Steve stands on a hardened crust of pahoehoe lava. Under this crust, the molten lava can stay hot for months. Breaking through is a real danger. Just standing still can melt your shoes.

I took my first photograph of Steve and lava.
"Steve, back up toward the lava … and smile."
"Hurry up!"
"Why?"
"My sneakers are melting."
Ouch! So were mine. Time to go. We ran to the helicopter and lifted off. As I stared back at the lava lake, I knew I'd be back.

How Volcanoes Form

The Earth's crust is made up of huge, solid chunks, called tectonic plates, that float atop Earth's molten mantle. Volcanoes form when magma from Earth's mantle breaks through the plates or oozes out at the edges. This can happen in different ways.

Subduction
When two plates smash against each other, one plate is forced under the other. The underlying plate melts into magma and can erupt through the overlying plate as a volcano. Central America's volcanoes, including Arenal in Costa Rica and Pacaya in Guatemala, were formed this way.

Mid-Oceanic Rift
When two plates drift apart, magma fills the gap between them and submarine (under the ocean) volcanoes can form. Iceland's Surtsey is a good example of a volcano that grew slowly until it emerged from the ocean.

Hot Spot
Sometimes there is a weak spot in one of Earth's plates and a stationary plume of magma erupts through it. The Hawaiian volcanoes were all formed this way.

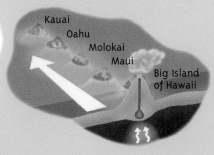

Kauai
Oahu
Molokai
Maui
Big Island of Hawaii

Fresh lava smells like burning metal. Here, it wipes out a road. I didn't know then that molten lava can be 1150°C (2100°F) when it erupts out of the earth.

NO PARKING

This pahoehoe lava was so hot I could only pose for a few seconds before running from the heat.

Everything came together for me that day — the science, the beauty, the thrill and even the danger. I was hooked. Steve and I returned to Boston but we longed to be researching volcanoes. We wanted to understand the secrets they held. We were determined to make this dream come true.

In 1987 Steve and I were married on the newest land on Earth — the lava that had oozed out of Puu Oo vent on Kilauea volcano. Instead of wedding slippers, I wore sneakers (in case we had to run). Instead of a veil, I had a gas mask. Our limousine was a helicopter.

A Hawaiian Hot Spot

The Hawaiian Islands were all formed by a hot spot under the Pacific Plate. Each island formed separately as the plate moved northwest over the hot spot at about the rate your fingernails grow — 36.5 mm (1.5 in.) per year. First came Kauai, then Oahu, Molokai and Maui.

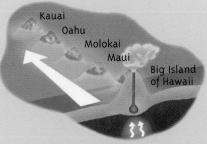

Kauai
Oahu
Molokai
Maui
Big Island of Hawaii

Now the Big Island of Hawaii sits over the hot spot that formed its six volcanoes: Kohala, Mauna Kea, Hualalai, Mauna Loa, Kilauea and Loihi sea mount. Kohala is extinct (it will never erupt again). Mauna Loa, Mauna Kea

and Hualalai are dormant (sleeping) but could erupt again. Scientists estimate little Loihi will have to be about 6000 m (20 000 ft.) tall before it even breaks the ocean's surface and becomes the Big Island's newest volcano, and that could take tens of thousands of years. Feisty Kilauea, still fed by the hot spot, is one of the most active volcanoes in the world.

Alone on Kilauea

Hot lava pours into the sea, causing a big steam cloud to rise as the seawater vaporizes. The waves pulverize the fresh lava into black sand, which washes ashore and creates a black sand beach. These beaches can form in a few hours and then wash away just as quickly.

In the three years since Steve's phone call, volcanoes had become my passion. And now I had come alone to Hawaii's Kilauea volcano, to photograph molten lava for a book about volcanoes. Also, I had to admit, I craved the excitement of being at an erupting volcano.

But Kilauea wasn't cooperating. Three times in two weeks I'd hiked out to the East Rift Zone, where the lava flows are sometimes visible, with no luck. The lava hid underground, leaving me nothing to photograph. Then it rained for seven days straight. By day eight, I had a severe case of cabin fever. Maybe I could catch a glimpse of the elusive lava at the coast, where Kliauea met the sea.

I zigzagged down the Chain of Craters Road to sea level and parked in front of a deep lava flow that had covered the highway — and several houses — a few months earlier. As I arrived, the sun broke through the clouds at last. I heaved on my backpack and climbed up the hardened lava rock.

Kilauea's lava flows originate high up on the flank of the volcano. Gravity sends the lava flowing down to the sea in red rivers. The chillier air quickly cools and hardens the tops of these rivers, creating sealed tubes through which the hot lava rushes. Shield volcanoes like Kilauea often form underground plumbing systems with dozens of these lava tubes. The tubes can be miles long.

Types of Lava

Molten rock below Earth's surface is called magma. Once it breaks through Earth's crust it is called lava. As soon as lava erupts, it begins to cool, causing gas in the lava to escape and minerals to crystallize and harden. The chemical composition, gas content and temperature all dictate what the lava will look like and how it will behave.

Viscous Lava
Viscous (sticky and slow-moving) magma of andesite, dacite and rhyolite sometimes plugs a volcano's vent like a cork. Then, pressure builds on gases trapped in the magma until ... *Kaboom!* A huge explosion occurs. (It's a bit like when you place your thumb over the opening of a soda bottle, shake it and release it.) The gases expand and explode violently, shattering the lava into smaller particles of cinders and ash.

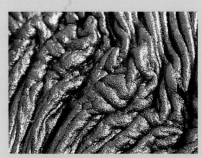

Pahoehoe Lava
Pahoehoe contains the igneous rock basalt and is hot and smooth. It moves like spilled pancake batter. When it hardens, it can be smooth or ropey.

Aa Lava
Aa also contains a lot of basalt, but it clumps as it cools. Aa looks like chunky blocks that have been lumped together in a long pile. When the flow moves, these blocks tumble slowly forward as if a bulldozer were pushing the pile from behind. The moving blocks make sounds like glass breaking and fingernails screeching on a blackboard.

Sometimes the lava tubes crack and red lava squeezes out. This is called a surface breakout. For a short period of time the red lava flow is visible, then it cools and hardens again.

A surface breakout is a rare and wonderful sight. I hoped to find one and photograph it before the lava hardened again. But walking around lava tubes can be treacherous. It's hard to know when you're right

I parked where the lava blocked the road. In some places the lava can be 18 m (60 ft.) deep.

over one, and the crust over a tube can be thin. You're at risk of breaking through and plummeting into the molten lava below. I planned to be careful, but I was also determined. I wanted to photograph molten red lava.

Here's an old photo of a young Steve standing inside an empty lava tube. Just imagine this tube filled with lava.

Hiking on lava? Don't forget to look down. One wrong step could be fatal.

To find my way back after sunset, I stuck white sticks into lava cracks about every hundred feet and tied white pieces of cloth to them like little flags. Later on, in the dark, the white markers would glow in my flashlight beam and lead me back to my car.

On my right, the coast dropped off sharply in a steep cliff. Saltwater droplets sprayed my face, and I could hear huge waves pounding the cliff. At high tide, the Pacific's waves were enormous!

I was thirsty. I needed some water. I sat down, but before I took a sip, I noticed that my seat was getting hot. I felt the hardened lava with the palm of my hand. It was hot. Very hot. Too hot. Uh-oh! Was I sitting right on top of a lava tube?

Hot cinders devastated part of a lush rainforest near Kilauea's summit.

Kilauea: A Shield Volcano

Shield volcanoes like Kilauea have surfaces that are cracked by earthquakes. These weakened areas are called rift zones. Kilauea has two rift zones: the Southwest Rift Zone and the East Rift Zone. For the last twenty years most activity has occurred along the East Rift Zone, which extends east from the summit to a point about 55 km (35 mi.) offshore.

Kilauea's East Rift Zone is walloped with up to a hundred earthquakes a day. They severely crack the rock in the area. As magma rises

from below, it exerts even more pressure on these shattered rocks. Finally, the pressure is too much. The rock cracks open, allowing molten magma to erupt to the surface. Rift zones aren't the only places magma erupts. It could surprise us and erupt in a new weakened area at any time.

Kilauea's fluid lava flows are so universally recognized that the phrase "Hawaiian type" eruption is an accepted scientific term used to describe similar volcanic activity around the world. Kilauea usually oozes pahoehoe or aa lavas, but a more explosive eruption is possible.

To get a better view, I hiked inland and scrambled up a mound of lava called a tumulus, a big pimple made when lava pressing up from beneath pops open, leaving a broken hill. From it, I could see an amazing sight. Steam and gases wisped up from the ground in crisscrossing lines. These were probably the outlines of lava tubes.

Off in the distance, I saw something even more amazing — a strange pink cloud. What was it? I wanted to investigate, but the gassy outlines of lava tubes were in my way.

Gases and steam can signal an underground lava tube.

I was looking for a route around the lava tubes when I came to a wall of lava rocks. I had stumbled upon Wahaula Heiau. A heiau is an ancient Hawaiian temple. Wahaula means "red mouth" in Hawaiian. Historians say that in the past human sacrifices happened here.

Some Hawaiian temples are considered sacred, and I certainly didn't want to disturb this one. Plus, it looked as though the lava tubes went under the heiau as well.

I was sandwiched between a raging sea cliff on the right and a sacred temple on the left. If I hoped to find out what was causing the pink cloud, there was only one way to go — straight across the tops of the steaming lava tubes.

Would the hardened tops of the tubes support my weight? There was only one way to find out. I held my breath and ran.

Volcano Types

Just like people, volcanoes come in all shapes and sizes. There are more than twenty-five different kinds of volcanoes on Earth. The lava's viscosity (stickiness) plays a big role in the type and shape of a volcano and how the volcano erupts. The stickier (more viscous) the lava, the more pointed and cone-shaped the volcano. The more fluid (less viscous) the lava, the more rounded and low the volcano. Here are a few of the most common types of volcanoes.

Shield Volcanoes

Shield volcanoes have very fluid basalt lava flows that can travel relatively quickly. Over time, thousands of syrupy lava flows can pile up like pancake batter to form these gently sloping, shield-shaped volcanoes. Kilauea is a shield volcano.

Stratovolcanoes

The classic Hollywood cone-shaped volcano is created as explosive eruptions of ash, lava and cinders build up in layers. Arenal and Stromboli are stratovolcanoes. Because the ash and lava form layers, these volcanoes are sometimes called composite volcanoes.

Compound Volcanoes

A compound volcano has frequent eruptions that form more than one cone, dome or vent. Pacaya is a compound volcano.

Cinder Cone Volcanoes

Cinder cones are formed when a vent (a hole through which lava erupts) tosses lava cinders and spatter skyward. When these fall back to Earth, they build an oval hill with a circular depression on top.

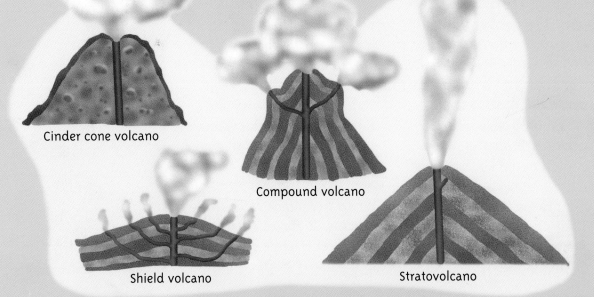

Cinder cone volcano

Compound volcano

Shield volcano

Stratovolcano

A Walk on the Wild Side

I ran across the smoking tops of the lava tubes as if my life depended on it. Because it did!

I made it … or had I? The pink cloud now loomed in front of me. And it was tossing chunks of lava right at me.

I had read about these steam clouds but never seen one. They happen when hot lava pours into cold seawater and instantly boils the water into steam. As it hits the cold ocean the hot lava is blasted into chunks called lava bombs and spatter. Huge explosions rocket the lava bombs higher and higher up into the scalding plume. Then, thanks to gravity, the heavy lava bombs and spatter hurtle back to Earth.

Most people would have run by now, but I wanted to see the lava pouring into the sea. That meant getting to the cliff edge. And *that* meant running right through the steam cloud — and the falling lava bombs.

I dodged and ran as hot lava bombs rained down around me. Blasts of steam blew some of the flowing lava into tiny shards of glass that pricked my bare arms like bee stings. Each step crunched. It was like running over black crystal snowflakes made of glass.

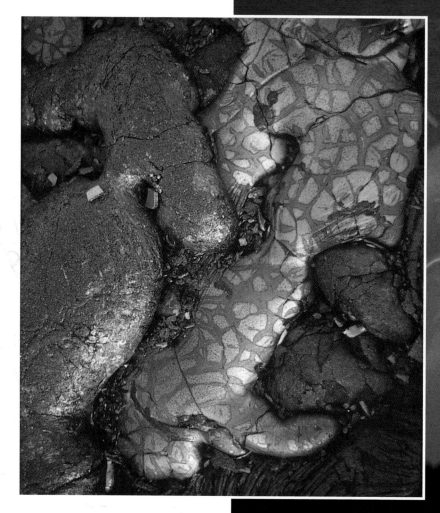

When pahoehoe lava cools quickly, it forms a crunchy black crust that shatters like glass if stepped on.

The pink cloud was made up of vaporized seawater, lava spatter and lava bombs. It was the bombs that worried me.

Two black lava tubes empty their molten contents into the Pacific Ocean.

The steam was hot. Worse, hydrochloric acid in the steam cloud stung my eyes, nose and throat. Coughing, I hastily poured water onto my bandana and tied it around my mouth and nose. I put on goggles to protect my eyes.

When I got to the cliff edge, I could hardly believe my eyes. Pounding waves had wrenched off a huge piece of the cliff. The lava tube and the entire river of orange lava was exposed as it poured into the ocean. But it wouldn't be visible for long. The cold seawater might seal the tube in minutes.

I grabbed my camera and began shooting. Ouch! The camera was getting hot. I wrapped the bottom of my shirt around the camera like a pot holder and worried that my film might be cooked.

I could see a small ledge jutting out about 2 m (6 ft.) down on the cliff face. If I could make it down there, I could get out of the heat. I carefully lowered myself. If I missed the ledge I'd boil in the lava/sea/steam cauldron below me.

I dropped onto the ledge and had a ringside seat for the best lava show in town. An incandescent torrent of fiery lava cascaded from a gaping tube in the black cliff and poured furiously into the turquoise sea. *Kaboom!* Another blast as hot lava sputtered into a whirlpool of steam. The noise was deafening.

The sun was setting and the light was magical. I began to shoot my film. I was lucky. It was almost twenty minutes before the sea won the battle and cooled the top of the lava river into a filmy black crust. The tube sealed over again and the show ended. The air grew still. All I could hear was the waves smacking against the cliff.

I took a deep breath and realized I might have been the first person to photograph this kind of volcanic event. I looked down and saw that my arms had a pink lava sunburn. I could feel my face glowing, too.

As I climbed back up, my left foot shattered the thin ledge I stood on. I could see pounding waves through the hole. Do not look down! Do not look down! I clung to the cliff face and heaved myself up. In the scramble, my leg caught on sharp lava, and it sliced into my calf muscle like a razor. I ripped a piece of T-shirt and tied a tight

HVO/USGS

Lava bombs are chunks of hardened lava. Some can be as big as a football — not something you'd want crashing down on your head.

A chunk of cliff fell off, exposing this beautiful lava river flowing from its tube. A rare moment, and one I was lucky enough to photograph.

tourniquet below my knee to slow the blood flow. Then I stuffed some absorbent photo lens wipes into the wound and duct-taped the whole thing tight to my leg.

In the dark the hike back was long. Thankfully my little white flags were there to guide me. When I got to the car I celebrated with a candy bar. The sugar gave me energy to drive the two hours to a clinic in Hilo.

The doctors cleaned my wound as well as they could, but to this day there are still tiny shards of lava embedded in my calf. Some people believe that lava is the physical form of Kilauea's volcano goddess, Pele. When my leg hurts, I wonder if that is true.

My lava sunburn was gone in about a week, and I was relieved that all my film was fine. Those dramatic images, one of which you can see above, were some of the hardest I have ever had to work to get. I feel that I really earned them. After almost twenty years of shooting volcanoes, they are still my favorites.

Some people leave offerings to the volcano goddess, Pele. It's good to have Pele on your side when you're on an erupting volcano.

The Other Side of Kilauea

Kilauea isn't all red lava and steam. Over 250 cm (100 in.) of rain soaks the top of the volcano, creating a green quilt of rainforest.

Giant koa and ohia trees form the forest canopy. Koa trees provide a habitat for many native birds and plants and so are extremely important to the health of the entire forest ecosystem. Ohia trees are common trees with uncommon beauty. Their feathery blossoms range in color from rare golden yellow to the more common deep ruby red.

The rainforest at Kilauea's summit is lush and misty. The hapuu ferns can grow to be 9 m (30 ft.) tall.

Giant hapuu and amaamau ferns thrive in the shade under the canopy. Ground-dwelling plants like palapalai and pukeawi dot the ground. The small, scrubby green bush lining many trails is the ohelo. Its berries are food for Hawaii's endangered Nene goose.

The ohia tree's blossoms range from pale yellow to bright crimson.

Hawaii's state bird, the endangered Nene goose, lives atop Kilauea volcano and eats ohelo berries.

The Really Big Bang: Arenal

Explosive Facts

Name of volcano: Arenal

Location: Costa Rica, Central America

Status: active

Type: stratovolcano

Height: 1657 m (5437 ft.)

Known people killed: about 100

S teve and I had been working together as a team for six years by 1992. We had begun to submit scientific reports to international organizations, such as the Smithsonian Institution's Global Volcanism Network, and to publish articles and photographs in magazines.

The more data and photos we got, the more we needed. Although Steve had been to several stratovolcanoes before we teamed up — Mount St. Helens in Washington State, Taal and Mayon in the Philippines, White Island, Ngaurahoe and Ruapehu in New Zealand — I had never worked at one up close. It was time for me to meet my first stratovolcano.

A big eruption of lava streams down the side of Arenal under a starlit sky.

Before setting out to climb Arenal, I stopped to take this photograph in front of its peaceful looking cone. Boy, was I in for a surprise when I saw Arenal erupt. I couldn't believe the force of the blast and height of the dark ashy eruption cloud. Arenal made Kilauea look humble.

Stratovolcanoes are far more dangerous than shield volcanoes. Instead of producing creeping lava flows, their eruptions explode with violent blasts of lava and ash. Some stratovolcanoes erupt continually. Others can sleep for decades, centuries or even thousands of years before unpredictably coming to life again.

We decided to travel to Central America, one of the most dynamic volcanic regions on Earth. Its west coast acts as a nursery for stratovolcanoes. Arenal volcano in Costa Rica was our first choice.

Imagine a wide, sunny valley with a river running through it. Farmers grow lush crops of coffee and bananas and raise chickens, pigs and cattle. Overlooking the valley is Arenal, a pretty, forested volcano crisscrossed with hiking trails and picnic spots. Serene, quiet, perfect — until the night of July 27, 1968. Then peaceful Arenal, asleep for 500 years, awoke and became a killer.

The first hint came when frightened villagers were slammed around their stucco homes by a series of violent earthquakes. Next, water in the nearby Tabacon River became warm, then hot, then almost boiling. Suddenly, a roar filled the valley and ... *Whoosh!* In just twelve seconds animals, farms, homes and seventy-eight people were buried under a deadly blanket of hot ash, gas and rocks. Arenal had thundered to life with the most deadly kind of eruption — a hurricane blast of scalding ash, lava and gas called a pyroclastic flow.

On the way to Arenal we passed many farms like this one, most with a few cows and coffee plants or banana trees. You can see the base of Arenal in the distance, its summit shrouded in clouds.

Arenal is still the most active volcano in southern Central America, and it continues to be a killer. Three people were caught in a small pyroclastic flow in 2000, and only one survived. Hikers have been killed by flying lava rocks and explosions of hot gas while trying to climb Arenal. No matter where you are on Arenal, you put your life at risk. And yet, because it is so active, Arenal offered us a chance to collect a lot of data in a short period of time. So in May 1992, we landed in San Jose, the capital of Costa Rica, five hours away from Arenal.

We set out on a splendid sunny morning. The car bounced and bumped along a rocky, dusty road, past dense rainforest, wild parrots and rainbow-billed toucans, until we reached the Tabacon River. After the rainy season, the river was very high, and there was no bridge. We assessed the situation. Steve took the wheel and gunned the engine in first gear. After a bit of engine sputtering, the car plunged across the 10 m (30 ft.) wide river, leaving a wake like a boat.

We arrived, wet and tired, at Arenal Volcano Observatory. The windowsill above the caretaker's small, cluttered desk held several jars. In the first was a pickled, red-banded coral snake. The second held a spider the size of a kitten, and the third a pit viper.

The caretaker grinned. "From here?" I asked.

He nodded vigorously, still smiling.

Pyroclastic Flows

A pyroclastic flow is Mother Nature's weapon of mass destruction. Also called a *nuée ardente,* a pyroclastic flow is a huge, scalding storm of gas, ash and volcanic debris that races down the slopes of a volcano at hurricane speed. The one you see here happened at Arenal.

Once unleashed, a pyroclastic flow leaves nothing in its destructive path. It can melt automobiles, level forests, bury entire cities and carbonize a human being in seconds.

A pyroclastic flow has a top and a bottom. Heavier rocks and big chunks roll forward like a giant burning wave along the ground while lighter ash and incinerating particles form a top layer called an upsurge. This upsurge can separate from the heavier bottom and leap ridges, fly uphill and even gust across large bodies of water, as if gravity had no effect on it.

(It was the lighter upsurge at Mount Unzen that killed the Kraffts. See page 7.) This superheated upper layer plows ahead of the heavy bottom debris, which flattens anyone or anything in its way.

The observatory was equipped with an outdoor observation deck built so high up that we could look *down* at the rainforest canopy. We watched a howler monkey, and it watched us.

Our one-room cabin had a glass wall facing the glowing cone of Arenal, so we could observe the volcano from indoors. But I was still thinking about those jars. I shook out the gray, stained mattress atop

While we were observing the volcano, a howler monkey was observing us. When the volcano exploded, he barked like a dog.

my wooden cot. A fat cockroach lumbered out, but no scorpions, poisonous snakes or spiders.

I doused the bed and floorboards with insect repellent and shook yellow sulfur powder onto the mattresses to discourage chiggers. Those pesky mite larvae burrow into folds of skin and itch like crazy. I'd already doused my clothes, socks and boots until they

were yellowish and reeked like rotten eggs.

From our bird's-eye view, Arenal's summit cone looked near enough to reach out and touch. By 8:00 AM we had set up our cameras, microphones, videos and journals. Then we watched and waited. We didn't have to wait long. Right before our eyes a huge, black, mushroom-shaped ash cloud erupted from Arenal's

Arenal volcano releases a small puff of smoke as Steve sets up his camera gear on the observatory deck. What a view!

cone. It looked stunning against the clear blue sky. I had just seen my first stratovolcano eruption!

Steve made detailed notes in his volcano journal.

I clicked away. Seconds later, the sound wave from the blast reached us. It sounded like the boom of a jet plane breaking the sound barrier. Arenal's was a dangerous beauty. The ferocity of the eruption gave me goose bumps.

We were lucky that day because the volcano erupted almost every hour. After a lunch of black beans and rice, Steve and I decided to be a little daring. We took our cameras and ventured up the volcano to take photographs and collect rock samples.

The quieter a stratovolcano, the more dangerous it is. Silence means it could blow at any minute. As we hiked up Arenal, it was unusually still. Deadly still.

My first stratovolcano didn't let me down. Arenal blasts a huge plume of ash, rock and debris into the atmosphere.

We photographed steam sputtering from the ground and grabbed a few rock samples. Then the mountain rumbled under our feet. It was time to get back to the observatory deck.

All day we were treated to blasts of ash that looked like giant sooty fists punching up into the clear blue sky. As the day wore on, I wore out, and the eruptions slowed. I finally staggered off to our cabin and instantly fell asleep, fully clothed.

Several times in the early morning hours, giant detonations jolted me upright, and every time my rickety cot collapsed, dumping me on the concrete floor with a thud. Finally I gave up and left the mattress on the floor.

Just after 5:00 AM the whole world seemed to explode. Arenal shot out a giant black cloud streaked with fire. Chunks of glowing rocks the size of refrigerators were tossed high into the air and came crashing down the mountain toward the

Calling All Field Assistants

Have you ever thought about working in the field with volcanoes? Volcano-watching can be very dangerous at times. It also takes a keen eye, an open mind and a lot of patience. Field assistants sit for hours in shifts to photograph, videotape and record in journals the onset of each eruption, the type of the eruption (ash, lava or steam) and the height of the eruption, estimated volume, intensity and duration. Back in the office, the data are entered into computers, and graphs are made to look for patterns or correlations or anything different or unusual. These detailed observations will someday be used to help unravel the secrets of how volcanoes work.

At Poas volcano in Costa Rica I had to wear a mask to keep volcanic particles out of my lungs. Volcano-watching can be a dangerous business.

observatory. Volcanic thunder boomed so loudly it rattled the windowpane. In the forest, birds screeched and howler monkeys barked like mad dogs.

Boom!!! Another massive eruption! This one sent a debris cloud nearly a mile high. I frantically looked around for Steve. Was he gone? No, there he was on the observation deck. I ran for him as the crashing eruption swept down the cone in our direction.

We watched in horror and disbelief as the burning, glowing wave swept over the area where we had been collecting samples just a few hours earlier. Within seconds, a tumbling mass of lava boulders, wildly spinning fragments and burning ash covered the spot. The ejecta tumbled closer but slowed as it smashed into the dense rainforest. Finally the eruption stopped and all was silent again, as if nothing had happened.

The flow had halted less than 400 m (1300 ft.) from us. The slope we

Stratovolcanoes

Stratovolcano magma is more viscous (thicker and stickier) than that of shield volcanoes. It can build up inside a vent, harden and plug the opening. Pressure builds from gas trapped within the magma. When the pressure becomes too great, the gas in the magma expands, blasting out the lava plug with a ferocious force. Thick lava is pulverized into smaller pieces of ash and volcanic cinders. As these fall they build a cone around the vent.

After an explosive eruption, sticky lava plugs the vent again until gas pressure builds and blows it out again. This happens repeatedly. Ash and cinders can alternate with lava flows and build up layers on the stratovolcano. Because of these layers a stratovolcano is sometimes referred to as a composite volcano.

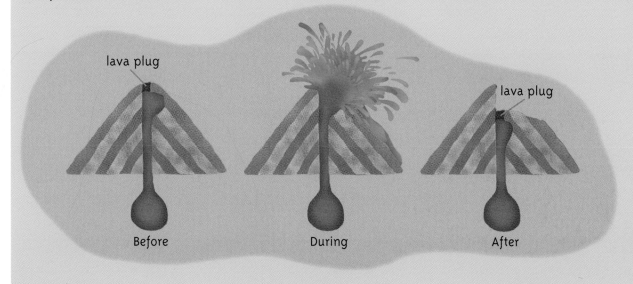

lava plug

Before

During

lava plug

After

had climbed had been pulverized by the eruption — there was nothing left. If we had stayed longer ... I shuddered at the thought.

In a brief twenty-four hours at Arenal, we had witnessed and recorded a staggering thirty-four eruptions. But nothing could have prepared us for the fury of that last one. We had collected a lot of data and photographs. And I had learned an important lesson: always respect a volcano, especially when it's quiet.

Arenal began our study of volcanoes in Central America. Now I was ready to take on yet another type of volcano. Next stop: Guatemala's compound volcano, Pacaya.

This is where we were headed — to the summit of Pacaya volcano in Guatemala.

Explosive Facts

Name of volcano: Pacaya

Location: Guatemala, Central America

Status: active

Type: compound

Height: 2552 m (8373 ft.)

Known people killed: unknown

Ai! Yai Yai Yai: Pacaya

Here we are in Guatemala, where more than the volcanoes are dangerous. Anti-government rebels, roving militias and armed guerilla fighters living in the hills make volcano-watching in Guatemala ... well ... challenging.

Guatemala City. From the air, it looks bustling. On the ground, the pollution and noise can be overwhelming.

On the way to Pacaya volcano we passed through lush rainforests that had a canopy of tall trees and an understory of smaller shrubs.

Why take on the added danger? Our friend Edgar Castro, who lives in Guatemala City, sent us a beautiful photo of Pacaya erupting a fountain of lava under a full moon. That photo was enough to convince us that Pacaya was worth a visit. Besides, we were curious to see how the eruptions of a compound volcano differed from those at Arenal and Kilauea.

The day before we were to climb Pacaya, we checked out the volcano's lower slopes. On the trail we spotted two rough wooden crosses lashed together. We asked a local worker what had happened. He pointed to Steve and said, "Gringo." Then he made a chopping motion with an imaginary machete. Next he "shot" me with an imaginary gun. A man and woman hoping to explore Pacaya had been robbed and murdered just one week earlier.

We spent most of the night discussing what to do. Should we forget the whole thing? Risk being murdered for our equipment and cash? Come back some other time? None of these options seemed very attractive, but we had traveled so far and hated the idea of giving up.

In the end we decided that if something happened to us, good or bad, we wanted to experience it together. After all, we were a team.

Before dawn the next day we left Guatemala City, with its exhaust-filled air, and headed toward Pacaya. We followed a hand-drawn map to the tiny mountain village of San Francisco de Sales to meet our guide, Luis.

Up and up spiraled the road, the lush green forest reaching out for us around each bend. The headlights caught a streak of black and yellow — a snake as thick as my thigh and longer than I am tall. Snakes? Bandidos? I hoped we had made the right decision.

Colorful villages like this one dot the route to Pacaya volcano.

church and a few tin-roofed homes. A delicious smell of roasted corn filled the air. A rooster jumped up on the hood of our truck and gawked in at us.

Women and small girls with honey skin and black, flickering eyes walked gracefully by. Each balanced a big basket on her head. They chatted while navigating the pot-holed road, yet the baskets stayed effortlessly in place. It was quite a balancing act.

Luis was a tall, thin man with a huge friendly grin. As he ducked back into his house, his small children peeked out at us. He returned with a knapsack and warm fresh tortillas filled with rice and beans for us. We eagerly took them and gave Luis some of our cookies and snacks. His children joined us and we had a quick, and very eclectic, breakfast. The tortillas were delicious.

Coffee workers carrying machetes walked barefoot along the road. In the surrounding fields, red coffee berries were ripe for picking.

Finally we pulled into the tattered little hamlet of San Francisco de Sales. There was one pretty stucco

Before we set out I try to envision being at the top of Pacaya volcano. I'm on the left and Luis, our guide, is second from the right.

37

The crater at the top of Pacaya looks like the mouth of a beast. We intended to go into its throat.

I looked up as I ate. The pink clouds parted and then, like a dinosaur, it appeared — the purple cone of Pacaya. Wow! Were we really going to the top? It looked a long way up. Then the clouds closed again like curtains and Pacaya disappeared.

Luis led the way. The trail to the top started in a vegetable garden behind his house. We climbed for hours. The exercise made us hot, and we were scratched by thorny bushes. Then — relief. We were engulfed in a blanket of cloud. The moisture felt good on my sweaty forehead, and the coolness made the climbing easier. We climbed right up through the cool cloud until, once again, we were exposed to the brutally hot sun.

After six hours of steady climbing we reached 2100 m (7000 ft.). I began to suffer leg cramps, a pounding headache and nausea. I was not getting enough oxygen from the thin air this high up. I needed to rest. We stopped and I had some water. Steve and Luis seemed fine. But as soon as we started up again,

How Big Is the Bang?

About sixty volcanoes erupt somewhere on Earth every year. Scientists who study volcanoes do not have accurate instruments to measure the size of an eruption, so reports of the same eruption can vary between different observers.

But volcanologists have come up with the Volcanic Explosivity Index (VEI) to help estimate just how big an eruption is on a scale from zero (weakest) to eight (strongest). Each interval is about ten times more explosive than the previous one. So, for example, a four is ten times more explosive than a three. One volcano can have a variety of eruptions that might all be rated differently.

The VEI is a guideline to measure how a volcano erupts, the volume of products exploded (lava, cinders, ash), how high the eruption cloud is, the type of the eruption and any other descriptive factors,

such as sounds, colors or smells. By recording eruptions during, say, a twenty-four-hour period, you can see how active a volcano is and track the nature of its eruptions.

No volcanic eruption in recent times has rated an eight. However, scientists theorize that the last eruption at Yellowstone volcano in the United States might have been an eight.

That eruption occurred about 640 000 years ago.

Only four eruptions have been rated a seven: Tambora, Indonesia, in 1815, which is also considered the deadliest eruption ever, killing an estimated 92 000 people; Baitoushan, on the North Korea–China border, in about 1050; Kikai, Ryukyu Islands, Japan, about 4350 BC; and Crater Lake, Washington State,

Elk graze amid the trees flattened by the eruption at Mount St. Helens in 1980. The blast had five hundred times the power of an atomic bomb. Geologists consider this a moderate eruption.

about 4895 BC. Mount St. Helens's eruption on May 18, 1980, has been rated a five.

my leg cramps got worse. I felt like I was climbing in slow motion, clumsily dropping one foot in front of the other. I could see the spasms in my leg muscles. I was sucking in air like a vacuum cleaner, but it still wasn't enough.

I stopped and sat down on the trail. We had reached an area called the Cerro Chino. From here I could see Pacaya's cone up close. A silent wispy puff of smoke whirled up from the point of the cone. I drank more water and decided I was never, ever, going to move again.

Of course I did, but the last 300 m (1000 ft.) were the worst. The cone's sides went almost straight up and were covered in loose, rubbly cinders. For each painful step forward, I seemed to slip back about five.

Steve and Luis were way ahead of me. I gave them the okay sign and waved for them to go up. I watched as they climbed up and over into the caldera at the top and disappeared. I sat down and wanted to cry. But what use would that be? I closed my eyes, took a few deep breaths and set out to finish what I had come for. I refused to let this volcano get the better of me. Forty agonizing minutes later I reached the summit, with Steve and Luis cheering me on.

Once at the top I couldn't believe the view. We were just inside the caldera where a gaping dark vent seemed to disappear into the center of Earth. Here and there among the cinders, steam whirled up. Down below, the tiny villages looked like white specks.

Luis had built a low wall out of big volcanic rocks for us to sit behind in the hope that it might offer some protection if Pacaya erupted. But the truth is, we were inside the volcano's cone and would not survive a big blast. We ate some bologna sandwiches and more bean-filled tortillas while we waited for Pacaya to do something. It did not.

It's impossible to predict when a volcano will burst into action. Surprise lava flows stream down the sides of Pacaya.

At the summit — finally — we were engulfed in toxic fumes, and a hurricane-force storm blew in.

Compound Volcanoes

A compound volcano has numerous cones, domes or vents formed when magma takes different routes to the surface. Picture a tree trunk with a few smaller branches. Magma is lazy and will search for the easiest escape route. It may flow freely from one branch for a while, but if that branch gets blocked it will find and flow from another. Each time there is an eruption, magma may find a new route, resulting in multiple cones, domes or vents.

Vesuvius near Pompeii, Italy, and Pacaya in Guatemala are both compound volcanoes. The Cerro Chino is an old cone on Pacaya's side.

Compound volcanoes are usually located where two of Earth's plates crash together. Because of this they tend to erupt more frequently than some other volcanoes.

But the weather did. Within a half hour, dark storm clouds moved in and the wind picked up to gale speed. We had planned to stay the night, but Luis said the storm would make that too dangerous. We were bitterly disappointed that we had come so far and now had to leave.

Discouraged and defeated, we started the long hike down, hoping to make the descent while there was still some daylight. By the time we reached the lower slopes the light was fading. I was exhausted and my legs felt like rubber. Now my main worry was the bandidos. We had been warned that bandidos roamed the slopes at night. As my flashlight beam caught trees and bushes, my mind played tricks on me. The shadows looked like crouching figures.

I wanted off this mountain, but we still had a long way to go, and most of it required hacking through thick rainforest. Luis told us to keep it quiet, but our thrashing sounded like a herd of buffalo on the move. In the dark everything seemed to go more slowly. It felt as if we had hacked our way through the entire country of Guatemala. Were we going in circles? Who knew? I just followed Steve's flashlight beam on the forest floor.

Three miserable hours later we heard muffled voices speaking in rapid-fire Spanish.

"Quick! Hide in the bushes!" Steve whispered.

I crawled under a scratchy bush, my heart pounding, trying not to think of snakes. Steve tossed more leaves and branches on top of me.

The voices got closer — at least five people — then shouting, running feet and bushes rattling. I heard Luis talking loudly in Spanish. What was going on?

Then Steve's voice: "Donna — come out, it's okay."

On jelly legs, I crept out of my hideaway. There was Steve with a group of equally scared geology students who thought we were the bandidos. After much hugging, laughing and crying, we descended the volcano with our new friends.

My legs recovered in a few days. The weather cleared so we set out for a second climb to the summit of Pacaya. On that second climb we did encounter bandidos and had to run down the mountain to safety. Thankfully my legs were strong enough to do it!

I had thought I was in good physical shape, but

Pacaya had proved me wrong. Since then, and to this day, I exercise every day with combinations of power walking, biking and rollerblading. On a volcano, being in excellent physical shape could save my life — and has.

Here's me on my rollerblades, wearing more protective gear than I do when climbing a volcano!

Volcano Watch International

When we returned from Pacaya, Steve and I moved from Boston to Volcano Village, Hawaii, atop Kilauea Volcano and founded Volcano Watch International. Our mission: to travel to Earth's active volcanoes and study how they erupt. Our goal: to better understand the nature of volcanic eruptions, so that we can help predict catastrophic eruptions and save people's lives.

Whenever we hear of a major volcanic eruption, we try to get there as soon as possible to photograph, videotape, write about and collect samples from it. Sometimes that means putting ourselves in danger. But if that is what it takes to save even one person's life, then our efforts will have been worth it.

We had achieved our dream. We were now a full-time international volcano-hunting team. I think we have the best jobs on Earth.

Fire and Ice: Stromboli

Explosive Facts

Name of volcano:
Stromboli

Location: Aeolian Islands, Italy

Status: active

Type: stratovolcano

Height: 926 m (3038 ft.)

Known people killed: about 120

My legs and feet felt numb. I was lying on sharp, cold rocks with only a light jacket over me as a blanket. My teeth were chattering so hard I bit through my lip.

Noisy blasts of lava rocketed up 500 m (1500 ft.) from one of the volcano's six vents. A bright blast of red lava streamers illuminated Steve as he built a crude rock wall to shield us from the flying lava rocks.

The volcano looms over the tiny village of Stromboli, where about 400 residents live year round. It seems quiet enough in this picture but don't be fooled.

Welcome to Stromboli, one of several volcanic islands in the Aeolian Island chain off the north coast of Sicily. We chose remote Stromboli because it has been erupting regularly for more than 2000 years. We hoped that by studying its frequent eruptions, we could field-test Steve's lunar correlation theory. Stromboli is also one of the most beautiful volcanoes on Earth. Its isolation and radiance inspired the ancient Greeks to call it the missing jewel in the Aeolian crown. It was the original home to the god Vulcan. Today Stromboli's dependable eruptions have earned it the title of the Lighthouse of the Mediterranean.

Explosive eruptions of lava rocket up to 450 m (1500 ft.) high from Stromboli volcano. It's a gorgeous sight — especially if you're up close.

After the coldest night of my life atop Stromboli volcano, I have never been so happy to see the sunrise!

We had picked a bad time. Italy and all of Europe were baking in a record-setting hot spell. The temperature at the base of the volcano was 44°C (111°F). The climb that should have taken us three hours took six in the heat. Shortly after reaching the summit, soaked with sweat, we were blasted with a freak cold storm that blew in from the west. The summit temperature plummeted to about 8 or 9°C (about 47°F). And now it was getting dark.

Villagers had warned us not to try to descend the volcano at night. Flashlights play tricks and make sheer black air look like solid rock. If we misjudged the terrain, we could easily fall to our deaths. We were trapped for the night.

We were perched perilously on a narrow ridge about 2 m (6 ft.) wide surrounding Stromboli's exploding crater. I peered 60 m (200 ft.) down into the very throat of the volcano. Six flaming vents glared back at me from the deep pit. I coughed as I gulped sulfur fumes.

The hot climb had left me dehydrated, and we were running out of water. I was groggy and disoriented. I took little sips, trying to make our meager water supply last the night, but I couldn't replenish the water I had lost.

What I didn't know was that I was also experiencing symptoms of hypothermia: shivering and sleepiness. Hypothermia is affected by three things: cold temperatures, wind speed and wetness. First your skin, fingers and toes get cold because surface blood vessels constrict and send blood to vital inner organs, such as the heart. Next the heart rate slows, which causes less oxygen to circulate. As your core body temperature drops, brain enzymes don't function properly and the brain's metabolic rate, which controls oxygen consumption, also slows. Without enough oxygen you become tired and confused. You shiver uncontrollably as your muscles spasm involuntarily in an effort to generate heat.

I was freezing. I shivered nonstop and felt so tired I just put my head down again on the cold ground. I couldn't think straight. The volcanic blasts seemed to be coming from far away.

My watch read 11:30 PM. I had been lying on the ground, cold, wet and shivering, for almost four and a half hours. When Steve began to shiver, too, we knew we were in trouble. It would be five or six hours before the sun rose, bringing warmth and the light we needed to get down off the volcano. I wasn't sure we would make it.

We only had a few calm moments at the summit before a storm blew in and darkness fell, along with the temperature.

Steve gave up monitoring the volcano, and we huddled together through the cold, windy night. We put our backpacks over our heads to protect us from flying rocks and nodded off between volcanic blasts.

When I awoke, I could feel sore depressions in my cheek from the cinders.

Stromboli's Deadly Legacy

No wonder the locals were worried about us. Stromboli is dangerous. Four people were crushed in 1919 by a 54 t (60 tn.) lava block. Three people were overcome by a pyroclastic flow and died in 1930. Another person was scalded to death in the hot seawater at the base of the volcano. A biologist was crushed by a large block of ejecta in 1986. In 1996 someone camping near the summit had his head crushed by a rock the size of a basketball. In 1997 a man fell 20 m (65 ft.) to his death trying to descend Stromboli in the dark. In

Sharp pieces of rock were tangled in my hair. I was desperately thirsty. I grabbed the water bottle and gulped down what was left. Far off in the distance I could see the black line of ocean and the ruby red horizon. The sun was about to rise. Thank goodness — we were going to make it.

1999 a blast burned three people at the summit. A woman was killed in 2000 by a flying rock. Also in 2000, a man killed himself by jumping into the 275 m

We never did get our lunar data on this frightful trip. We were lucky just to make it back alive. I swore that, after spending the worst night of my life atop Stromboli, I would never return there again.

But fate had other plans for me.

(900 ft.) deep, fiery mouth of Stromboli. Dozens of other people have been severely injured and burned by flying rocks and debris over the years.

Just eighteen months later, I was struggling up Stromboli volcano again. We'd been offered an opportunity we couldn't pass up. The National Geographic Society (NGS) wanted to fund an expedition to Stromboli, and they wanted to make a movie about us at work photographing and studying the volcano. Their generosity gave us an incredible chance to field-test Steve's lunar correlation theory and get some amazing pictures.

So here I was about to summit Stromboli again. In addition to the NGS film crew of four, we had two field assistants with us — Larry Mitchell from Texas and Chris Cobb-Smith from the United Kingdom. Although we had trained our assistants to collect data, this would be the first time either of them had seen an explosive volcano up close.

Here I am with the National Geographic Society film crew arriving at the dock in Stromboli, ready for a new adventure.

Moon Magic

Our goal for the Stromboli expedition was to test the theory that the Moon can influence volcanic eruptions on Earth. Steve had been investigating this lunar correlation theory for more than a quarter century at volcanoes all around the world.

Once a volcano becomes active (begins erupting), Steve believes that, under the right conditions, it is possible to use the Moon's tidal influence on Earth to predict when larger-than-normal eruptions, or more frequent eruptions, are most likely to occur. (He is not saying that every time there's a full moon a volcano will erupt somewhere on Earth.)

Predicting volcanic eruptions is difficult, and many factors are involved. The Moon's tidal influence on Earth is just one of these factors. (Right now, few, if any, scientists are using the Moon's influence in their prediction models.) If the Moon does affect volcanic eruptions, Steve wants to understand how it does and by how much. This knowledge can then be used with traditional scientific methods to help better predict when a volcano could erupt catastrophically.

For the Stromboli expedition, Steve had made a table of predictions as to when we might expect the biggest or most frequent eruptions to occur at Stromboli.

Also, during our stay, the Moon would pass its perigee — the point in its orbit when it is closest to Earth — just three days before the full moon. Steve believed that the coincidence of these two factors (perigee and full moon) would lead to a period of intense volcanic activity.

To document the volcano's activity, we had to detail every eruption, recording its height, content (ash, lava, steam, gas), sound and color. We also had to record anything unusual that preceded or came after the eruptions,

such as a peculiar odor or rockfall within the vents. We would also photograph and

videotape as many eruptions as possible. Our notebooks, film and tapes

Does the Moon influence volcanic eruptions here on Earth? We hoped to discover the answer.

became more valuable than jewels to us.

Once the expedition ended, I input all the data into our computer and Steve reviewed it to see if the size of the volcano's eruptions followed his predictions.

What did we find? Just as Steve had predicted, activity increased after first quarter moon. It culminated within twenty-four hours after lunar perigee, with the biggest and most audible blasts occurring halfway between perigee and full moon. Activity dropped significantly after the full moon. We were on to something!

The plan was to monitor the volcano in pairs twenty-four hours a day, seven days a week, beginning April 1, 2001 (first quarter moon), to April 16, 2001 (last quarter moon), with the full moon in between. The Moon would be at perigee (the point in its orbit when it passes closest to Earth) near the time of the full moon. We wanted to see if volcanic activity increased around that critical time.

We would set up camp on the outer lip of the summit crater. From our base camp, we would climb a berm of fallen volcanic cinders. Once over this mini-mountain, we would arrive at our monitoring stations inside the lip of the summit crater. We would have front row seats to one of the most dangerous shows on Earth.

Some Strombolians were superstitious and told us we were crazy to stay atop the deadly volcano for fifteen days. As far as we knew, our expedition team would spend the longest amount of time ever on this volatile volcano.

Our tents at NGS base camp wouldn't offer us much protection against the volcano — or the storms. But they would be home sweet home for two weeks.

Steve poses with Volcano Watch International field assistants Larry Mitchell (middle) and Chris Cobb-Smith (right). Even though they know the risks, Larry and Chris are ready to go back to Stromboli at a moment's notice.

At noon on Monday, April 2, Steve and Larry headed out for their first six-hour monitoring shift. The plan was to work in pairs so that if one person was hurt, the other could help or radio base camp.

At 5:30 PM Chris and I set out for our first shift and met Larry and Steve coming down. They had filmed, photographed and written down details of some impressive explosions and data during their shift.

As Chris and I climbed up the loose cinders with our heavy packs, we sweated through our clothes. Then the sun set and the temperature dropped. Our packs thudded onto the tiny ledge inside the lip of the volcano that would be our monitoring station for the next six hours. The cold and the precarious perch seemed all too familiar.

I couldn't believe it! Within an hour, my horrible Stromboli nightmare had returned — with a vengeance. I was freezing and Chris was also numb to the bone. He joked that his trips to Siberia had been warmer than this!

Got Gear? A Shopping List

Visiting a volcano? You need the proper gear! Here are a few of the things I had to buy for our Stromboli expedition: climbing rope, custom-fitted pantsuits treated with fire retardant chemicals, several hundred multicolored glow sticks to mark a path in case of an emergency, five cases of batteries, waterproof hiking boots, tents, personal hygiene shovels (bright orange), bullet-proof safety goggles to protect our eyes from blasts of sharp rocks and ash, backpacks, construction helmets to protect our heads from rocks falling from the blasts, gas masks and filters, a medical kit with burn supplies, headlamps, indoor tent booties, sleeping bags, water bottles, warm jackets, pants, cameras, digital video camera, two-way radios, lenses, tripods, flashes, metal carrying cases and film, camera

vests, and even special socks to wick away moisture and keep our feet dry and warm. Whew!

Field assistant Charlene Meyers has got gear!

At 11:30 PM we were so cold I called an end to the shift. Stiffly, we descended to base camp. Larry and Steve replaced us. They spent a miserable, freezing night before returning at 6:00 AM.

We realized we had to change the monitoring schedule. With six-hour shifts, none of us was getting enough sleep. Although it would be more risky, we voted to try individual shifts. I would do an eight-hour daylight shift and Steve, Larry and Chris would alternate monitoring at night. The downside was that if something happened, we would be on our own.

We hung in this way for almost a week, although Stromboli seemed intent on defeating us. We were hit daily with 90 km/h (55 m.p.h.) winds, poisonous gases and blinding whiteouts. Then on Saturday, April 7, 2001, our "luck" changed — for the worse.

I returned from my shift cold, exhausted and filthy, looking forward to our evening meal of hot pasta. The winds had picked up and were whirling acidic ash into my face. Lightning flashed, and pitch-black clouds gathered at the horizon. It looked as if a big storm was going to blow right through our base camp.

The Moon was approaching perigee — an important time for testing our theory — but safety was more important. We decided it was just too dangerous to do the next shift, so we told Larry and Chris to hunker down in their tents. The NGS film crew had descended to the village below.

Once the storm blew in, we were in a complete whiteout of ash and lethal fumes.

By sundown Steve had more bad news: our two-way radios were not working. Steve, Chris, Larry and I were alone on top of the volcano, a massive storm almost upon us, with no way to communicate with each other or the rest of the world.

By 11:00 PM a howling, hurricane-force wind trapped Steve and me in our tent. I didn't dare look outside. I could only hope that Larry and Chris were safe in their tents.

Around 1:00 AM I heard a huge *r-r-r-rip!* A piece of our tent had torn off, and if we didn't fix it, the whole tent might go, too, with us in it. Steve struggled outside to patch the tent poles only to discover they had snapped in half. He could barely stand against the wind and hail. He yelled that he was going to drag over some heavy equipment to weigh down our tent.

The tent floor was still flying wildly, so I braced my back against the side to keep it down. No luck. The buffeting of the wind tossed me up and across the tent like a leaf. Finally Steve dragged enough weight over to hold the tent down, at least for now.

Steve braced himself next to me. The wind was deafening, and every half hour or so we heard a massive *Boom!* from the volcano. We crossed our fingers and waited it out. We hoped that Chris's and Larry's tents were holding strong.

The storm raged on. Then at 2:00 AM Chris came to our tent, screaming something over the wind. It took a while to get the whole story. Without telling us, Chris had gone up to the summit. He returned, windblown and freezing,

with a notebook full of detailed eruption data, taken during the critical lunar perigee. Chris's data were helpful in strengthening Steve's lunar theory, for which we are grateful. We are even more grateful that he is alive today.

The next morning our camp looked as if a bomb had gone off. The tents and supplies were in tatters. Food and equipment were everywhere. I dug some oranges out of the ash and squeezed juice for the four of us. Steve found some boxes of cookies. Slowly, we put the camp back together. The NGS film team returned, and filming

continued. But Stromboli didn't let up. Strong winds and foul weather plagued us for the duration of the expedition.

Refusing to let Stromboli defeat us, we stuck it out on the summit for two solid weeks and collected a lot of good data. When all was done, we came home with over 570 detailed descriptions of the eruptions we had seen. We analyzed the data and found we had new evidence to support Steve's lunar theory. And we were alive to share our amazing adventure with the world. We had faced Stromboli and survived.

After fighting the storm I was so exhausted I could barely keep my eyes open.

A Lifetime with Volcanoes

As this book goes to press, Steve and I are still collecting data at other volcanoes to further test Steve's lunar theory. Our research will keep us busy for years to come. So far, the results look promising.

I consider myself lucky to do the work I do. Technology has done wonders to advance scientific investigation, but sometimes it makes science feel clinical. That's why I love studying volcanoes. You have to be there, watching and listening to them. There are things I can see, smell, feel, taste and hear at an active volcano that I cannot get from even the best digital movie, computer screen or scientific instruments. The power and the beauty of a volcano are something you just have to see first hand.

I wrote this book because I love to share the wonder of volcanoes with others. So I pass the torch to you, the new generation of volcano explorers. Who knows, maybe one day you'll study volcanoes and change scientific thinking. You might discover a vital but missing clue to predicting volcanic eruptions — and saving lives.

As for me, I hope I am still climbing volcanoes when I am eighty. I can't imagine life without them. I'll see you on the summit. Dress warmly!

I am off again for a long hike to Kilauea's Puu Oo vent. Maybe our paths will cross along the trail?

Glossary

aa: a type of lava with a coarse, blocky texture that breaks up and solidifies into a jumbled mass of broken rocks called clinkers

ash: dust-sized volcanic particles ejected in an explosive eruption

basalt: a type of dark, igneous rock found in some lava that oozes from fissures rather than explodes

caldera: a big circular depression at the summit of a volcano that is created when the summit suddenly collapses. This happens when magma drains rapidly away from the main magma chamber under the summit.

cinder: a small piece of lava with a gray, ashy color

cinder cone volcano: a hill made of cinders and other erupted fragments that pile up around a volcanic vent

composite volcano: another name for a stratovolcano

compound volcano: a volcano that has two or more vents and/or domes either at its top or on its sides

crater: a bowl- or funnel-shaped depression at the opening of a volcano or vent. A crater is smaller than a caldera and may be caused by an explosive eruption.

crust: the thin brittle outer layer of Earth

dome: a steep-sided mound of viscous lava that slowly expands as it is fed from below

fissure: a crack in Earth out of which lava may erupt

Hawaiian-type eruption: a usually non-explosive eruption of fluid lava. Thin layers of lava gradually build up, creating a gently sloping shield volcano.

lava: molten rock erupted onto Earth's surface, where it cools, solidifies and forms new land. Molten rock beneath Earth's crust is called magma.

lava bomb: a large glob of semi-hardened lava that erupts from a volcano and remains round or football-shaped even after it hits the ground

lava lake: a pool of lava over a volcanic vent or a depression

lava tube: an underground tunnel that forms when the surface of a lava flow cools and crusts over. Molten lava flows inside the tube.

magma: molten rock beneath Earth's crust. Once molten rock breaks through the crust to Earth's surface it is called lava.

mantle: the molten region of Earth's interior below the crust

pahoehoe: extremely fluid basalt lava that solidifies into smooth or ropey shapes

pyroclastic flow: a deadly eruption of super-hot volcanic ash, chunks of rock and gases that races down a volcano like an avalanche, incinerating everything in its path

shield volcano: a volcano with gently sloping sides, created from multiple layers of fluid lava

spatter: a ragged splash of fluid lava spit out of a vent. Spatter clots are smaller than lava bombs.

stratovolcano: a steep-sided, cone-shaped volcano composed of different types of lava flows, ejected fragments and pyroclastic flows that build up over thousands of years

vent: the opening through which a volcano erupts molten rock, ash and gas

volcano: a cone, hill or mountain that forms around a vent as volcanic material is expelled and builds up

Index